Nomads & Travellers

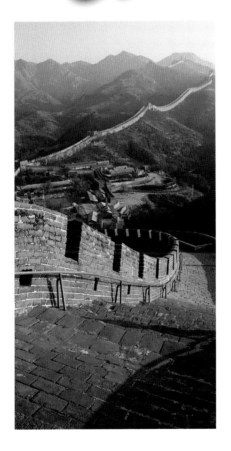

DAVE DALTON

www.heinemann.co.uk/library
Visit our website to find out more information about Heinemann Library books.

To order:
 Phone 44 (0) 1865 888066
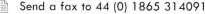 Send a fax to 44 (0) 1865 314091
 Visit the Heinemann Bookshop at www.heinemann.co.uk/library to browse our catalogue and order online.

First published in Great Britain by Heinemann Library, Halley Court, Jordan Hill, Oxford OX2 8EJ, part of Harcourt Education.
Heinemann is a registered trademark of Harcourt Education Ltd.

Editorial: Jilly Attwood and Kathy Peltan
Design: Ron Kamen and Celia Jones
Illustrations: Jeff Edwards
Picture Research: Ruth Blair and Kay Altwegg
Production: Séverine Ribierre

Originated by Modern Age
Printed and bound in China by South China Printing Company

The paper used to print this book comes from sustainable resources.

ISBN 0 431 01384 5
10 09 08 07 06
10 9 8 7 6 5 4 3 2 1

British Library Cataloguing in Publication Data
Dalton, Dave
Nomads and Travellers
 (People on the Move)
 305.9'06918

A full catalogue record for this book is available from the British Library.

Acknowledgements
The publishers would like to thank the following for permission to reproduce photographs:
[Alamy Images **p.9**(Bryan & Cherry Alexander), **p.17**(Jiri Rezac); Bridgeman Art Library **p.33**; Corbis **p.13**, **p.8**(Peter Johnson), **p.11**(Penny Tweedie), **p.15**(Reuters), **p.16**(Steve Kaufman), **p.20** (DiMaggio/Kalish), **p.24**(Annie Griffiths Belt), **p.27**(David T. Grewcock; FLPA), **p.28**(Jonathan Blair), **p.40**(Strauss/Curtis), **p.43** (Lou Dematteis/Reuters), **p.45**(Galen Rowell); Corbis(Harcourt Index) **pp.26, 31**; Panos Pictures **pp.4, 6, 30, 39**, **p.5**(Chris Stowers),**p.10**(Penny Tweedie), **p.19**(Giacomo Pirozzi), **p.21**(Ahikam Seri), **p.35**(Karen Robinson), pp.**37**(Paul Weinberg), **p.41**(Penny Tweedie), **42**(Paul Weinberg).

Cover photograph of a man and his camel, in Rajasthan, India, reproduced with permission of photolibrary.com.

The publishers would like to thank Angus Willson, Director, Worldaware for his assistance in the preparation of this book.

Every effort has been made to contact copyright holders of any material reproduced in this book. Any omissions will be rectified in subsequent printings if notice is given to the publishers.

Disclaimer
All the Internet addresses (URLs) given in this book were valid at the time of going to press. However, due to the dynamic nature of the Internet, some addresses may have changed, or sites may have changed or ceased to exist since publication. While the author and Publishers regret any inconvenience this may cause readers, no responsibility for any such changes can be accepted by either author or the Publishers.

Contents

Words in bold, **like this,** are explained in the Glossary.

chapter one

Introduction

Always on the move

When we talk about people on the move we usually mean **migrants**. Migrants move from one place to another. Once they have moved they usually settle down permanently. But this book is about people who never stop moving. Their way of life is **nomadic**.

Nomads

Why are nomads always on the move? They have to move because they rely on a source of food that moves, or on foods that appear at different places as the seasons change. Nomadic ways of life include **hunter-gatherers, pastoralists,** and **shifting cultivators.** We will see what each of these means in the following pages. All nomads are on the move, but that is all they share. Nomads have adapted to a wide range of different **environments.** They have developed many different ways of life.

Nomadic people are often traders. A nomad takes his goods to market in Mauritania, Africa.

Travellers

Travellers are also always on the move, but they move around in a country that is mostly occupied by settled people. They supply something that settled people need or want. These working travellers are not an alternative to the settled **economy**, but a necessary part of it. We will see some of the ways in which this works.

People have always travelled for fun, for religious reasons, or to see the world. But it is only in modern times that large numbers of people been able to afford to travel so widely. Millions of people now take foreign holidays. Sometimes they go abroad several times a year, and to exotic destinations. Millions more people travel for business reasons. But they are not the kind of travellers we will look at here.

Threatened lifestyles

You will find that many of the descriptions of nomadic ways of life in this book are written in the past tense. Some nomadic people, and nomadic lifestyles have disappeared or changed for ever. Their languages, myths, beliefs, customs, and crafts are lost. Others are under threat. We will see why, and how nomadic people can respond.

Travelling light

People who are always on the move must limit their possessions to what they can carry with them. How much that is depends on whether they travel on foot, or have pack animals, horsedrawn vehicles, or motor vehicles. But it will always be less than people who stay in one place. If you are on the move all the time, many things are difficult or impossible to make. Nomads often have quite simple **technology**. This is partly because they must carry everything, and partly because they never have the chance to develop more complicated technology. They are too busy moving. Nomads and travellers who have links with settled people get a lot of the things they need by trading with them.

The lives of travellers, especially traditional nomads, might be simple, but their culture can be as rich as any other. And nomads have adapted ingeniously to some very difficult environments.

Consider this: hard choices

Imagine you belong to a group of nomads that has to move on every day. What does the group do when someone is ill, or has an accident, or dies?

These temporary migrants from Indonesia are working on a plantation in Malaysia. They have travelled from their homes in search of work.

Ninety-nine per cent of human history

Nomadic ways of life are ancient. Millions of years ago, all humans were **hunter-gatherers**, hunting animals and gathering plant food. We were all nomads. We moved around with the herds of animals we preyed on. We moved with the seasons, as food appeared in one place or another. Once hunter-gatherers have eaten all the food in a particular area, they have to move on to find more.

Hunter-gatherers everywhere

As humans spread out across the world from their first home in Africa, they took the hunter-gatherer way of life with them. It was a slow **migration**, for three reasons. First, it was at walking pace, up to 5 kilometres (3 miles) per hour. Second, there was no rush. People would only move on when the population reached such a level that there was not enough food. Third, as people entered new **environments** they had to learn about them. What was good to eat, what was poisonous, which animals were dangerous, how could they catch the **game**, and what should they do about shelter and water? Until they fully understood how to make the most of the new environment, they would not be able to live there in large numbers. Over tens of thousands of years, humans found ways to live in every part of the world they could reach.

The hunter-gatherers who painted this scene on the wall of a cave lived in what is now the Sahara Desert in Libya.

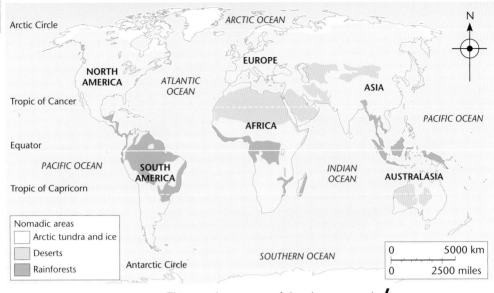

This map shows some of the places around the world where nomads still live.

Farming

About 10,000 years ago, people started to learn about farming. They discovered how to grow the plants that were best to eat, and tamed and herded food animals. In this way, they were able to produce more food.

Once they had sown a crop, farmers had to tend it by weeding, watering, and keeping off the pests. Then they had to harvest it. The amounts of harvested food were too big to be carried around, and soon it was time to sow the next season's crop. As farmers now needed to stay in one place, they built more permanent homes. Now some of the people could be spared from farming to do other things. For example, a skilled potter could make pots all the time, and exchange them for food. The pace of invention and **technological** change got faster.

Hunter-gatherers in the margins

The places where farmers lived and grew their crops were not empty. Hunter-gatherers had been living there for thousands of years. But farming will nearly always displace hunter-gathering, for reasons that we will look at later. People following the older way of life either changed to the newer way, or moved away to a place where there was no farming. The migration of farmers into new land caused another migration, of the hunter-gatherers.

Eventually farming became so widespread that the ancient hunter-gatherer way of life was pushed into the margins. This usually meant places where farming was too difficult. Over a few thousand years, hunter-gathering changed from being the only way for humans to live, to being a rare way of life, confined to a few places. Today, most people live settled lives.

chapter two

Hunters and gatherers

Sand and ice

In this section we will look at the contrasting ways of life of two **hunter-gatherer** groups, in two very different **environments**. They are the San of southern Africa, and the Inuit of the Arctic. Both ways of life are described in the past tense, because they have seen many changes in recent years. But the San and the Inuit people still live in their harsh environments, and some of them still pursue their traditional way of life.

The San People

The San people (formerly known as Bushmen) live in several countries of southern Africa. They live in an area where farming is impossible, the semi-desert of the Kalahari, which is mainly Botswana. The main food of the San was the highly nutritious mongongo nut, which came from a **drought**-resistant tree. They also knew of another 84 species of food plants, although they normally used only 23 of them. There were 54 edible animals, of which the San regularly hunted seventeen. The women gathered plant foods and the men hunted. A group would travel about 10 kilometres (6 miles) a day searching for food. They moved their camp about five or six times a year, but never more than about 20 kilometres (12 miles).

The San's way of life needed only very simple **technology**. It rarely gets cold in the Kalahari, so they didn't need many clothes, and they made simple shelters of branches and leaves. They could find the food they needed with only a few hours' effort each day. However, there is only enough food in a semi-desert area to support a very small population.

San mothers on the move, with their children and possessions.

The Inuit

The Inuit live in the Arctic, where winter lasts nine months and only 50 days each year are frost-free. Their traditional way of life was based on hunting and fishing, with big differences between the seasons. The Netsilik Inuit, living near Hudson's Bay in Canada, were living this way as recently as the 1920s. In winter they hunted seals. They lived in igloos, houses made of snow. By July the ice had melted, and they moved inland. Here they lived in tents, fished for salmon in the rivers, and hunted caribou. They made clothes from the skins of the animals they caught. They also made their kayaks, harpoons, sledges, and igloos. Their winter clothes had to be warm enough for the hunters to survive hours waiting by a seal's breathing-hole in the ice, ready to harpoon the seal when it came up for air.

Most Inuit people now use modern technology, such as snowmobiles and rifles. Many of them now live in conventional houses and have given up their traditional way of life.

An Inuit man in Greenland is fishing from a kayak. He is throwing a harpoon.

Consider this:
population control

Hunter-gatherer populations were very low because their environment could only support a few people. The old, injured, or sick might be left to die. If the group moved every day, women had to carry any children who were too young to walk. As they could not carry two children, they could not have a second child until the first could walk. For this reason, and also to stop the families getting too large, they sometimes killed newborn babies. Mothers and fathers had to make difficult decisions. If not, everyone might have gone hungry.

The Aboriginal people of Australia

When white European explorers first reached Australia in the 18th century, there were about 750,000 Aboriginal people living there as **hunter-gatherers**. They had developed many different ways life, to suit the many different **environments** in that vast country.

This map shows the different climate and vegetation zones in Australia.

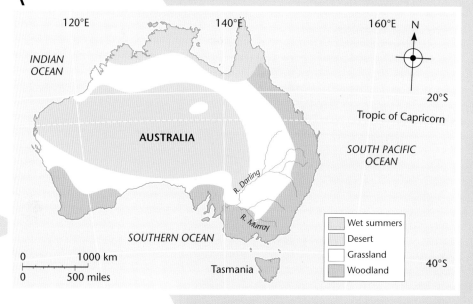

Dry land

Australia is the driest continent on Earth, apart from Antarctica. It has an unpredictable pattern of **droughts**. The Aboriginal people adapted to this by keeping their population low, so that they had plenty to eat in good years and enough to survive in bad years. They also learned to make use of a wide variety of food plants, so that if one failed they could use others. If food ran out in one place, they would simply move to another place where there was food.

As well as adapting to their environment, they also managed it by controlled fires. These had several benefits. They drove out animals that could be killed and eaten immediately. They turned dense thickets into open parkland, through which people could travel more easily. The parkland was also an ideal habitat for kangaroos, the best **game** animal in Australia. The fires encouraged the growth of new grass, which fed the kangaroos.

Wetlands

The far north of Australia has a climate with a wet season of heavy rain, and many wetlands. The Gidjingali people who lived there moved with the seasons, to find different food sources as they became available. In the wet season, when the swamps were full, they ate waterlilies. They ate the stalks raw, made the seeds into cakes, and cooked the roots. In the early dry season they moved to an area where they could find large yams. Later they moved to the edge of the wetlands, where the men hunted geese and the women dug up the roots of rushes. At the height of the dry season, they ate the nuts of the cycad tree. These are very abundant, but poisonous. The Aboriginal people had various ways of getting rid of the poison, to make the nuts edible.

Technology and culture

The technology of the Aboriginal people included barbed spears, tools made of bone and of ground and polished stone, and **boomerangs.**

Aboriginal people knew several ways of starting fire, and had discovered sewing. They used hooks and nets to catch fish. They also had a rich culture, with more than 250 languages and trade routes across the whole continent. They painted on cave walls and on bark, and made rock carvings. They had music, song and dance, myths about their origins, and spiritual beliefs.

See page 32 to find out what happened to the Aboriginal people after Europeans settled in Australia.

Fish

Australia's biggest river system, the Murray-Darling, is in the south. There the Aboriginal people dug canals, to enable eels to get from one marsh to another. They caught the eels in traps. Traps at different levels in the marsh came into operation as the water level rose and fell with the seasons. It was hard work to build the traps, but they produced a lot of food.

These Aboriginal people are in a cave in Rembargua, in Australia's Northern Territory. The rock painting on the cave wall is of a kangaroo.

case study:

Native Americans

North America is bigger than Australia. It has an even greater variety of **environments**. Native Americans there developed many different ways of life, each well adapted to their environment.

Forest people

In the great forest of the east and north of the continent, people lived by hunting beaver, deer, rabbits, and porcupines. They used bows and arrows and travelled in birch-bark canoes. They collected berries and other plant foods, and lived in bark shelters. There were also many farming people in clearings in the forests of the east and midwest. They grew maize, beans, and pumpkins, and added meat to their diet by hunting. They had no **domesticated** animals, either to eat or to pull ploughs. Tribes in the midwest left their villages for months at a time during the hunting season. They set up temporary homes in **wigwams**.

Buffalo hunters

The Great Plains between the Mississippi River and the Rocky Mountains were **grassland**. Here the climate was extreme, with very hot summers and very cold winters. The Plains were home to millions of buffalo, and the Native Americans of this huge region lived by hunting them. For many thousands of years, the people of the Plains killed buffalo by driving them over cliffs. They ate as much meat as they could while it was fresh, but also dried and smoked the meat to store for hard times. They also hunted other animals, and collected plant food.

This map of the Great Plains shows the location of the different tribes of Native Americans.

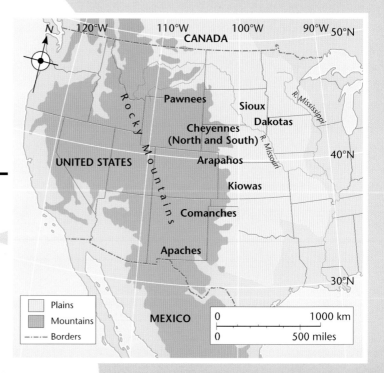

When the Spanish arrived in the **New World** in the 16th century, they brought horses. Some of them escaped, and rapidly spread across the Great Plains. The Native Americans tamed the horses and became skilled riders. Now they hunted buffalo on horseback, with bows and arrows. The horses also helped them to carry their possessions as they followed the buffalo herds. Horses pulled a pair of long poles with one end dragging on the ground called a *travois*. Possessions were carried on a platform supported on the poles. When the people set up camp, the poles were used to support the **tipi**, a tent made of buffalo skins. As settlers began to arrive on the Great Plains, Native Americans were able to buy rifles from them. Rifles made their hunting even more effective. Even so, they only killed as many as they could eat. They took fewer buffalo than the natural replacement rate of the great herds.

For a few generations, a distinctive and successful way of life flowered on the Great Plains. There was plenty of food, and plenty of spare time to spend in rituals, war with other tribes, and decorating all the buffalo-hide possessions.

This family from the Southern Cheyenne tribe were photographed with their *travois* in 1890.

Consider this:
contact

At first, the Native American people benefited from the arrival of settlers from Europe. The hunters of the northern forests sold furs to European traders, and bought from them iron cooking pots, steel knives, and guns. The buffalo hunters of the Great Plains benefited from the horses and rifles. But pp 32-33 show how the nomadic life of the Native Americans eventually ended because of contact with settlers.

case study:

The indigenous people of Amazonia

In the dense **tropical** rainforests of South America, Africa, and Southeast Asia, there are people who live by hunting and gathering. Some of them also practise a kind of farming that is specially adapted to the forest **environment**. Amazonia in South America is the biggest single region of tropical rainforest in the world.

Amazonia

Amazonia covers most of the area drained by the River Amazon. It is hot all year round, and there is a lot of rain. A huge number of species of plants grow here. They support countless insects, reptiles, birds, and mammals. Until very recently, the rainforest was too dense for outsiders to enter, except by boat along the rivers. The **indigenous** people continued their ancient way of life in isolation.

The forest provides fruit, berries, nuts, and roots. There are fish in the rivers, and eggs to be collected. Hunters use blow-pipes with poison darts to bring down animals from the trees overhead. Tribes that live by hunting and gathering move on when they have used up the local food sources, and may also move with the seasons.

Amazonia is a huge area of rainforest in Brazil and neighbouring countries, that is home to many indigenous people.

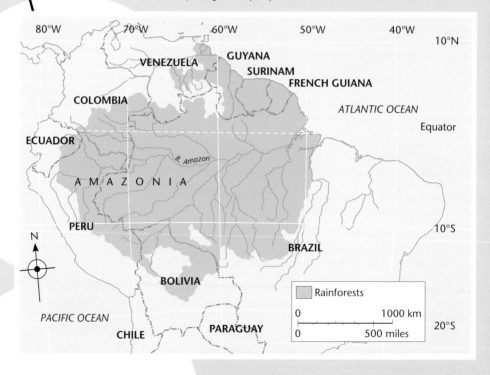

Contact and isolation

The indigenous people of South America have been in contact with European colonists and settlers for 500 years. Some of the tribes in Amazonia are there because they retreated into the forest from their original homelands, to avoid settlers. Outsiders gradually found their way into the rainforest, for example during a brief boom in tapping wild rubber trees in the 19th century. Some white settlers now live a sort of hunter-gatherer lifestyle, tapping wild rubber trees and collecting Brazil nuts. But some tribes living in their traditional places have only been contacted by outsiders very recently.

Sometimes the people of Amazonia settle in villages, such as this one, Yawallapiti.

Shifting cultivation

Many tribes also farm, using a method called **shifting cultivation**. They clear a small area of forest, sometimes by controlled burning, and grow crops. The richness of a tropical rainforest is held in its vegetation. Living plants grow in the decomposed remains of dead plants. There may be only a few centimetres of topsoil in a tropical rainforest. The fertility of this soil is soon exhausted, so the farmers clear a new garden every two or three years. They leave the land to grow back as forest and regain its fertility naturally. They have to move home whenever they clear a new garden. As long as they have a big enough area of forest to move around in, they do not use any piece of land too often. One tribe, the Yanomami, who live in the hills along the border between Brazil and Venezuela, grow around 60 crops. About 20 are for food. The rest are for medicine, making everyday objects, or other purposes.

A fragile environment

The hunter-gatherer and shifting cultivation ways of life support only very small populations. The rainforest is a fragile environment, with thin, infertile soil. It cannot support more people in the long term. Recently settlers have attempted to farm more intensively in Amazonia. They have quickly used up the fertility of the soil.

chapter three

Pastoralists

Following the herds

There are many places in the world that are too dry, rocky, or cold to grow crops. The **pastoralist** way of life makes the most of even these difficult **environments**. Pastoralists keep herds of animals, and travel around with their herds as the animals move to find fresh grazing and water.

Following the reindeer

The Saami people of Arctic Scandinavia rely on semi-wild herds of reindeer for their survival. They cannot control the wanderings of the reindeer as they search for food, but they do control single animals. They milk the females. By **castrating** males, they make them more manageable. They can then use them to pull sledges carrying their possessions. They eat the meat of the reindeer, and use their skins for clothing and tents. There are about 60,000 Saami, but only 10 per cent of them are reindeer herders nowadays. Many tribes of Siberia, in Russia, also rely on reindeer. They may also hunt other animals for meat or furs.

This herdsman of the far north is a member of the Chukchi tribe. He is herding reindeer in Chukotka, Russia.

Taming the herds

Most other pastoralists have **domesticated**, or tamed, the animals they herd. Over many generations they have controlled the animals' breeding, to encourage useful changes. They prefer sheep with heavier fleeces, and cattle that give more milk. Pastoralists also look after their herds. They protect them from predators, and lead them to good **pastures** and water. In this way the land can support more animals, and more people, than if it was left to wild animals.

Consider this: settled shepherds

Not everyone who keeps cattle or sheep is a nomad. Where the land is not too mountainous and the climate not too extreme, farmers and their animals can stay in one place all year round.

Pastoralists do not have to spend time, and take risks, hunting for meat. They can choose an animal to kill when they want. And they do not have to kill the animals to make use of them: they can have milk every day, and a fleece every summer.

Moving with the seasons

In mountainous parts of the world, the higher pastures are snow-covered in winter. Herds spend the winter in the valleys, and by spring they have eaten all the grass. As the snow melts on the higher land, it reveals good grazing. The herdsmen move the animals to higher pastures, and often stay with them all summer to protect them from wild animals. In autumn they take the herds back down into the valley.

This seasonal to-and-fro is called **transhumance**. In some places it involves long and difficult journeys for the whole community. In Iran, the Bakhtiari people take their herds of sheep and goats over the six ranges of the Zagros Mountains in spring. They cross the mountains again on the return journey in autumn. They climb passes that are 3650 metres (12,000 feet) high, and cross rivers that are in flood with the melting snow. And they do all this on foot.

Protecting against risks

Even when protected by their owners, animals face many risks. They may be killed by predators, infected by disease, or die of hunger or thirst if there is a **drought** and the grass stops growing. A risk to the herds is a risk to the people who rely on them. Pastoralists usually try to protect their livelihood by building up the numbers of animals in their flock and herds. With a large herd, even if many animals die in a bad year, enough survive to make it possible to build up the herd again.

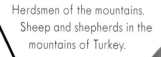

Herdsmen of the mountains. Sheep and shepherds in the mountains of Turkey.

case study:

The Maasai

About one third of the land area of Africa is grassland with occasional bushes and trees. It is called **savannah**. Rainfall is extremely seasonal and highly unpredictable, so it is difficult to grow crops. **Nomadic** herding is the most practical way of life. Around 10 million herders of cattle, sheep, and goats occupy a vast zone of savannah, stretching from Senegal to Somalia and southwards to Kenya and Tanzania. One of these nomadic groups is the Maasai.

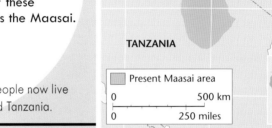

The Maasai people now live in Kenya and Tanzania.

Way of Life

The Maasai people originated near Lake Turkana in what is now northern Kenya. They moved south in the 19th century, and clashed with the British when they **colonized** Kenya. Many Maasai died from the disease smallpox, and their cattle suffered from a disease called rinderpest. Early in the 20th century, the British moved the Maasai to an area on the border with what is now Tanzania. There are now about 300,000 Maasai living there. This territory is also home to the wildlife that people go on safari to see, such as zebra, giraffe, and lions.

For the Maasai, cattle are what make life good. Milk and meat are their best foods. They also keep sheep and goats, and use donkeys for transport. Their everyday food is milk, and when other food is scarce they also draw blood from the neck of their cows to drink. They only kill cattle for meat on special occasions. They get most of their meat from sheep and goats. In the past, they aimed to live by their cattle alone, and buy other foods, but today they also grow grain and other crops. They move their herds from one place to another to find fresh water sources, and to give the grass a chance to grow again. Traditionally, everyone in an area shared access to the water and **pasture**.

Problems

In the past, the biggest problem for the Maasai was unreliable rainfall. Without rain there would not be enough grass to keep their herds healthy. Their solution was to move around widely, to find areas where rain had fallen and grass had grown. But in recent years the problem has changed. Their freedom to move around has been reduced, as the best land has been taken over for private farms and ranches. The government has also set aside other land for wildlife parks.

The Maasai can now graze their herds only on the driest and least fertile land. Even if these areas have enough grass to feed the cattle, the soil is damaged because the herds cannot be moved on to give the land a chance to recover. Well-intentioned governments encourage the Maasai to sell off many of their animals, and settle in private plots. This makes it even more difficult to survive a **drought**, because the land is not good enough. It also undermines the Maasai's traditional nomadic way of life. Many Maasai have given up and found jobs in nearby towns.

Consider this:
a protected species

The savannah has distinctive wildlife: zebra and other grazing animals, and lions and other predators. These are protected by wildlife parks and provide a lot of income from the tourists who come to see them. But these parks have been created by taking land away from the Maasai people. Should the Maasai, and their traditional way of life, also be protected?

In order to survive, the Maasai need to move their herds to fresh grazing areas. But now their freedom to move across the savannah is under threat.

case study:

The Bedouin

Across huge areas of North Africa, Central Asia, and the Middle East, there are desert areas where it is too dry for cattle. Instead, people herd sheep, goats, and camels. They often also earn a living by trading goods across the deserts. They buy goods from the settled people on one side of the desert, and sell them to settled people on the other side. People who live like this include the Tuareg of Mali, Algeria, Libya, and Niger, and the Bedouin of North Africa and Arabia.

The Bedouin

Bedouin people live in desert and semi-desert areas, where pasture and even water are in short supply. They often rely on underground water sources, which they reach by digging wells. When the water is used up, the group must move on.

Bedouin live in tents made of cloth, woven from the hair of goats by the women. When the tribe moves, the women are in charge of dismantling the tents, packing them on the camels, and reassembling them at the new site. The sides of the tent can be rolled up so that a cool breeze enters, or staked down to make the tent secure in a sandstorm.

Like most **pastoralists**, the Bedouin rarely eat meat, because this would reduce the size of their herd. They get milk, cheese, and yoghurt from their animals, and also eat dried fruits, dates, rice, and wheat. They sell rugs, cheese, milk, goats, and camels to the settled people at the end of the desert. And they buy things that they need but cannot produce themselves, such as cloth, jewellery, flour, rice, tea, sugar, and coffee.

Adapting to the desert

The Bedouin have adapted to life in the hot, dry desert in several ways. They wear layers of loose clothes to protect them from the Sun, wind, and especially dust and sandstorms. They ride camels, because the distances they have to cover are too far to walk. They have a tradition of hospitality to strangers, because without it travellers might die, and anyone might need to travel.

The inside of a bedouin tent is made comfortable with colourful rugs which the Bedouin weave themselves.

A child shepherding his sheep in the Judean desert. He is from the Jahaleen tribe of Bedouin. They settled here in the 1950s after being driven out of the southern Negev desert.
Then this area was part of Jordan, but since 1987 it has been part of Israel.

Settling down

Not all Bedouin are completely **nomadic**. Even in the desert there are oases – areas where there is a permanent source of water. Some Bedouin have settled in oases, where they grow crops as well as keep animals. Others have left the harsh nomadic lifestyle and settled in towns, or have adapted to modern **technology** and drive pick-up trucks rather than riding camels. But they often keep parts of the Bedouin **culture**, for instance putting up a tent in the grounds of a conventional house.

Separate tribes

Because pasture for the animals, and water for animals and people, are so scarce and far apart, freedom of movement is essential to the Bedouin way of life. But the Bedouin do not wander aimlessly. They plan their movements according to the seasons, and each tribe stays within its traditional territory. Each tribe guards its territory closely from other tribes.

Consider this:
trade and ideas

Nomads like the Bedouin are well placed to be traders as they are used to travelling great distances and live in the deserts between thickly populated and prosperous areas. The Tuareg people of the Sahara Desert traded goods between settled people in North Africa and West Africa. Ideas and beliefs often spread along these trade routes. Islam started in the desert of Arabia and nomadic, trading people spread Islam into many areas of Africa and Asia.

chapter four

Travellers

Different kinds of travellers

Travellers are people on the move, not because they are **hunter-gatherers** or **pastoralists**, but because of a whole range of other reasons. In some cases travelling is the traditional way of life for a whole group; sometimes individuals adopt a mobile lifestyle for all or part of their lives. On these two pages we will see some of the main kinds of travellers. Later in this chapter we will look in more detail at some of them.

Seasonal work

Most farm work is done by the farmer, his or her family, and permanent workers who live on or near the farm. But in many kinds of farming there are seasonal peaks of work, when extra help is needed. These include sheep shearing, picking fruit and vegetables, harvesting grain crops, and lifting potatoes. Groups of workers travel around the countryside doing this sort of work.

Traders

From the 18th century to the middle of the 20th century, many goods were carried through Britain on canal barges, or around the coasts on small boats called coasters. The people who ran the barges and coasters lived on board. They went wherever there were cargoes to be taken. The great rivers of Europe and North America still carry a lot of goods. The barges are home to floating families, who travel with their cargoes.

Floating families photographed on their barges in London, 1931.

Seasonal fishing

Even some fish have seasons. When there were huge shoals of herring in the North Sea, the fishing fleet followed the shoals in their seasonal migration. The women who cleaned and gutted the fish followed the fishing fleet up and down the east coast of Scotland and England. The women were known as 'herring lassies'.

Services

Other travelling people provided services. Tinkers mended pots and pans, in the days when these were expensive items to replace. People travelled door-to-door offering to sharpen knives and scissors. Perhaps the most popular service that travelling people provided, and still do provide, is entertainment. Wandering minstrels, jugglers, magicians, Punch-and-Judy shows, even small travelling theatres, would set up in the marketplace for a day or a week. When everyone in the town had seen the show and thrown their pennies in the hat, the show would move on to the next place. Circuses and funfairs continue the tradition, following a circuit so that they arrive in each town at a set time every year. The rides, food stalls, games of chance, and fortune-tellers are entertaining for a few days, but most people would not want to go to the funfair every week.

Peddlers

In the 18th and 19th centuries, peddlers travelled around the countryside selling their wares door-to-door. They sold small, portable, luxury items that people would not buy very often. Peddlers had to cover a big area, so as not to return to any one place too soon. As towns and villages grew big enough to support weekly markets or permanent shops, the peddling way of life died out.

Consider this: travellers need settlers

Travellers rely on settled people as customers. Without them, they would not be able to keep their way of life. Each community can respect the other. People appreciate differences when they know and understand them.

case study:

The Roma

The travellers described in the last section were mostly individuals who chose a wandering lifestyle, or followed the family way of life. But there is a larger group of people who are probably the most typical wanderers of all. They are the gypsies, or Roma. Here we will look at their origins and traditional way of life.

Origins and destinations

The Roma left India about a thousand years ago, and reached Europe in the 14th century. The first record of Roma in England dates from 1550. They speak a language called Romani, which is derived from ancient Punjabi or Hindi. They have added words from all the countries they have passed through since they began travelling. People who have studied the Romani language can work out the routes they took. The Roma have migrated to parts of Asia and Africa, the **New World**, Australia and New Zealand, but above all they are in Europe, and especially in Eastern Europe. They make up 10 per cent of the population of Slovakia, 8 per cent in Bulgaria, 6 per cent in Romania, 5 per cent in Hungary, and 2 per cent in the Czech Republic. The world population of Roma is about 12 million.

Strangers

Wherever they travelled, the Roma seemed strange and exotic to the settled people. Their name in many European languages, such as 'zingari' in Italian, or 'zigeuner' in German, comes from a medieval Christian group in **Asia Minor**. The English were equally confused about where the Roma came from. The English word 'gypsy' comes from 'Egyptian'. The Roma's language, their beliefs, their appearance, and their way of life were different, and it was hard for a settled community to get to know people who were always moving on.

The Roma way of life

Roma travelled in beautifully painted horse-drawn caravans called vardos. They stopped to camp in open spaces by the roadside. Today they are more likely to use modern caravans pulled by pick-up trucks, but they still like to have horses around them.

Getting together

Roma usually travelled in small groups of two or three families. But they would get together every year, in big gatherings. In Britain, they would meet up at the Appleby Horse Fair in northern England. In France they would join the **pilgrimage** to Saintes-Maries de la Mer in the Camargue, in the south of France.

A Roma family travelling in their caravan to the annual Appleby Horse Fair in Cumbria, England.

Roma made their living in many of the ways described in the previous section. They were tinkers and horse dealers, and in modern times they combine these two traditions by breaking up old cars for spare parts. The women carved wooden clothes pegs and made lace, and sold them door-to-door. The men sharpened knives and did seasonal farm work. Gypsy fortune-tellers are a feature of funfairs, and the Roma of Spain and Eastern Europe are famous for their music.

Settling down

Today many Roma have settled down, though they still keep parts of their distinctive way of life. Eighty per cent of Hungary's Roma no longer speak Romani at all. The Roma have formed an international organization, and they have their own flag and anthem. They hold World Roma Day on 8 April. You can read more about the issues facing the Roma on page 34.

Consider this: fear and envy

Settled people have mixed feelings about the Roma. Some envy the freedom and excitement of their way of life, and they have fascinated writers and musicians. They also arouse fear and suspicion. If Roma people are around when a crime is committed, local people might be tempted to blame them.

Modern travellers

Nowadays, many people do a lot of travelling, for both business and pleasure. Three groups of people do even more travelling: young people who have not yet started their working lives; older people who have retired from work; and people known as New Age travellers.

Backpackers

Many young people take a 'gap year' between school and university, or before they start a career. They cram everything they think they will need into a backpack, and set off to see as much of the world as they can, until they run out of money or time. Some volunteer to do something useful for those who are less fortunate, either in their home country or in a poor country. Others choose to do paid work, at home or overseas. Or they may join an expedition to a faraway place, and learn a new skill on a training course. In 2003, 26,000 people from the UK took a gap year before university, and 20,000 took a gap year after university.

A new industry

So many people now take a gap year, that an industry has grown up around them. There are companies that will make the arrangements for people who want to do voluntary work abroad. There is also special backpackers' accommodation in the favourite destination countries. These include Australia, New Zealand, and Thailand.

Retired people

Many people retire from work while they are still active. Some have enough money to do the travelling they did not have time for during their working lives. s. Some retired people in the USA take up a seasonal pattern of travelling in their own country. In the winter they move to warmer states, such as Florida and Arizona. Then they return home for the summer.

A backpacker sets off on his travels.

They are known as snowbirds. Older people from northern Europe may do something similar, spending the winter on the warmer coast of the Mediterranean Sea. Some of these seasonal travellers own a second house in their winter home.

New Age travellers

Many backpackers and snowbirds can travel because of the relative prosperity of their home countries. Another group of people in prosperous countries, known as New Age travellers, have taken up a nomadic way of life over the past 40 years. They travel in old buses or converted vans. They choose not to have a permanent job or a permanent home. They have rejected the way of life of the majority of people in modern society.

New Age travellers often convert old buses so that they can live in them. They are modern versions of the traditional Roma caravans.

New Age values

New Age people have different values from those of most people in modern prosperous countries. They often reject conventional politics in favour of peaceful, direct action. They are against war, poverty, racism, and big business. They are concerned about the **environment**. They may take direct action against road building, quarrying, tree-felling, and other actions that damage the environment. Many choose not to eat meat, and to use traditional methods of health care.

Seasonal workers

Many people become travellers in search of work. Some jobs are only available at certain times of year, so people have to travel to find them. There are many kinds of seasonal work. These pages look at two main kinds: picking fruit and vegetables, and jobs linked to tourism.

Pickers and processors

When fruit ripens, the farmer must get it picked quickly. Picking fruit is hard to mechanize. Machines cannot yet judge the ripeness of fruit, or handle it gently enough. The farmer employs seasonal workers for a few weeks, until all the fruit is picked. These workers then move on, to pick another crop.

Every May, 300,000 Polish peasants cross the border into Germany to pick asparagus and strawberries. Britain allows in 25,000 seasonal workers, mostly from Eastern Europe, to pick fruit and vegetables. Different crops have different harvesting times. Workers can move on from strawberries to raspberries and then blackcurrants in the early summer. In late summer they pick plums, apples, and pears. There is also work in the packing sheds, and in the factories that freeze the fruit and vegetables.

The USA

Huge numbers of seasonal farm workers work in the USA's vineyards, orchards, and farms. They may spend the winter in Florida, picking oranges and grapefruit. They then work their way up the east coast as far as Maine, harvesting tomatoes, potatoes, and apples. By the time the apple harvest is over in Maine, it is time to return to Florida again.

Another route takes workers harvesting vegetables from southern California northward through the Pacific coast states. In California they pick grapes for the wine-making industry, as well as cotton, salad crops, and oranges. Some of these **migrant** workers are American citizens of Mexican descent. Many others are **illegal immigrants** from Mexico.

Routes taken by cowboys driving cattle to market in the American west.

Hard work

There are many kinds of seasonal jobs, but they are nearly all unskilled, low-paid, often outdoors, and involve long hours of hard work. These conditions are acceptable to students or backpackers. But most seasonal jobs are taken by **economic migrants** from poor countries, like the Mexicans in the USA. They can earn more doing seasonal work than they could at home. It also gives them a chance to get into the USA, where they may find a better, permanent job, and settle as long-term immigrants.

Tourism

Another industry which needs huge numbers of seasonal workers is tourism. Seaside holiday resorts are busiest in the summer, ski resorts are busiest in the winter. They all need waiters, bar staff, kitchen workers, cleaners, lifeguards on the beaches, and ski instructors on the slopes.

Seasonal workers from Mexico picking oranges in Florida. When they have picked all the oranges, they will move on.

Cowboys

Farmers also need to get their animals to market. This provided seasonal work in the American west in the 19th century. Longhorn cattle bred on the plains of Texas had to be taken 2400 kilometres (1500 miles) north to the railways at Abilene or Kansas City. The cattle were driven by cowboys. The era of the cattle drive did not last long. When settlers started to farm the Great Plains, and the railways reached closer to the remaining ranching areas, the drives were no longer necessary.

chapter five

The issues

Co-operation and conflict

Nomads and settled people have contrasting ways of life, but they do not live in isolation from each other. At the boundaries people may live in partly nomadic, partly settled ways. Settled and nomadic people may co-operate with each other, or come into conflict.

Co-operation

The most common form of co-operation is trade. Often each way of life produces more than they need of some goods, and none of others, so trade benefits both groups. In a good year, with plenty of rain and grass, **pastoralists** have a surplus of animals, which they exchange for grain with nearby farmers. Prosperous settled farmers also welcome expensive luxuries that the mobile nomads bring from far away.

At markets like this one in Mali, Africa, pastoralists and settled people exchange their products, and nomadic traders sell their goods.

Competition

Nomads may compete with settled people over land. In a **drought**, pastoralists may move their herds on to farmland to find grass. If the rains are good, farmers may try to grow crops on land that the pastoralists usually graze. The boundary between the two ways of life moves back and forth with the pattern of wet and dry years. A similar effect happens if individuals and families switch between ways of life according to the weather. But over a long period, the difference between farming and pastoralist areas, and ways of life, is clear.

Conquest

If conflict breaks out between nomads and settled people, nomads have some advantages. Their mobile way of life is suited to a military campaign. Experience of fighting between nomadic tribes over grazing land and water also makes them better prepared for warfare than peaceful settled people. There are many examples in history of nomadic people invading, defeating, and destroying great empires.

The fall of the Roman Empire

Invasions by tribes from Central Asia destroyed the Roman Empire. Horse-riding nomads armed with bows and arrows, such as the Huns, invaded and destroyed the Roman Empire in the 5th century. When these invaders found themselves in land that was good for farming, they settled down as farmers themselves. England was invaded by the Jutes, Angles, and Saxons from north Germany and Denmark in the 5th century. They too settled down in their new home.

The Great Wall of China

Nomadic people also attacked China. The Chinese Emperor had built the Great Wall to defend his country against attacks. Nevertheless, nomadic tribes from the plains of Mongolia and Central Asia invaded and conquered China in the 13th century. The Mongols led by Genghis Khan and his descendants, ruled an empire that stretched from China to eastern Europe in the 13th and 14th centuries.

The Great Wall of China was built to protect settled people against nomadic attacks.

Settling down

When nomads conquered a settled people, they did not turn the settlers into nomads. They often settled down themselves. Two nomadic nations settled down in large numbers. The Magyar people occupied the area we know as Hungary, at the end of the 9th century, and became farmers. They were seeking safety after attacks by other nomadic people. The Ottoman Turks came from Central Asia. In the 13th century they came to **Asia Minor**. They settled down and created the country which we now know as Turkey.

An unequal contest

In more recent conflicts between **nomads** and settled people, settled people had advantages that made them more likely to win. There were more of them, and they had more resources and better **technology**.

The Great Plains

By the mid-19th century, the nomadic Native American buffalo hunters of the Great Plains had developed a way of life perfectly adapted to their **environment**. But they were using land that white settlers from the eastern USA wanted. When it came to battle, the nomads were using spears and bows and arrows against the guns of the US army. The settlers were also better organized, and had the railway and the telegraph. Native Americans suffered badly from diseases caught from the settlers, because they had no immunity. They also had no tradition of drinking alcohol. When settlers sold them alcohol, it had a devastating effect. Many became addicted to it. The settlers shot the buffalo for their hides, and soon came close to wiping them out. This was probably the hardest blow to the Native Americans, whose whole way of life relied on the buffalo.

As the Native Americans were cleared off the Great Plains into **reservations**, ranchers with huge herds of cattle took their place. But the ranchers, too, soon came into conflict with the next wave of settlers, who ploughed up the grass to grow wheat. The government gave farmers a legal right to their land. The farmers put up fences to keep out the cattle and cowboys. Cattle ranching continued in the mountains, but on the Great Plains the settlers had won.

California

There were about 200,000 Native American **hunter-gatherers** in California before white settlers arrived. They were split into hundreds of tiny tribes, such as the 2000 Yahi of northern California. Armed white settlers

almost wiped out the Yahi in four massacres between 1866 and 1868. A few survivors hid themselves in isolated canyons for more than 40 years. The last known Yahi survivor, Ishi, was discovered in 1911, and died in 1916.

Australia

By 1988, 200 years after the beginning of European settlement in Australia, there were about 170,000 Aboriginal people. Since 1788 their numbers had fallen by more than 75 per cent. About half of them were living in towns and cities, and many were working on farms. Only a few were still following the way of life of their ancestors.

Like the Native Americans, the Aboriginal people suffered from diseases and alcohol brought by the settlers. As the good land in Australia filled up with European settlers, the Aboriginal people were pushed off. By 1988, only about 10 per cent of the land legally belonged to Aboriginal people, and that was the least valuable or useful land.

Armed white settlers also attacked and massacred Aboriginal people. All the original people of Tasmania were wiped out. The last survivor, Truganini, died in 1876. As recently as 1928, white people killed 31 Aboriginal people in the Northern Territory. Since then, Aboriginal people have fought for their rights in Australian courts, and won. Australians have realized that wrongs were done to them. Aboriginal people have gained citizenship, land rights, and respect for their ancient **culture**.

Degraded, subdued, confused, awkward and distrustful, ill concealing emotions of anger, scorn, or revenge, emaciated and covered with filthy rags; these native lords of the soil, more like spectres of the past than living men, are dragging on a melancholy existence to a yet more melancholy doom.

A visitor to Australia in the 1830s described the Aboriginal people he saw.

Consider this: into the margins

Defeated nomads get pushed into the margins. They may survive on land which no settler could want, as Aboriginal people did in the deserts of Australia. Or they may take on the settled way of life, and lose their identity and culture.

The Native Americans won this battle of Beecher's Island, usually known as Custer's last stand, in 1868. But they were eventually defeated and forced into reservations.

Fear and persecution

When travellers come into conflict with settled people, it is not because they are competing over land or other resources. Very often, there is a clash of **cultures**.

Mutual suspicion

Travellers and settled people benefit **economically** from each other. The travellers offer useful services, and settled people offer their money. Farmers get their crops picked, and seasonal workers earn a living. But the two groups can have a wide range of attitudes to each other. At best there is mutual respect and tolerance. Settled people may admire the freedom of the traveller lifestyle, but they may also resent that freedom. Travelling people, here today and gone tomorrow, can be seen as untrustworthy, suspicious, and even frightening. Travellers look different and have different beliefs. For many people, what is different is also dangerous.

Some of these attitudes may be reflected in the travellers' feelings about settled people. They may feel contempt for their customers, even as they sell to them and entertain them. Travellers are outnumbered by the people they move among. They may feel vulnerable, and that can lead to fear.

The Roma

The Roma are the most distinctive of travelling people, and have suffered harassment and occasional violence ever since they reached Europe. In the Second World War (1939–1945) Germany invaded Eastern Europe, where many millions of Roma lived. The German Nazis considered Roma to be 'sub-human'. One estimate is that they killed 1.5 million Roma in the gas chambers of Auschwitz and other death camps.

The Roma remain a large minority in many countries of Eastern Europe, where most have adopted a settled way of life. Nevertheless, the majority of the population still **discriminates** against them. These are the results of an opinion poll held in Romania in 2003:

- 93 per cent said they would not accept Roma as members of their own family
- 46 per cent do not accept the presence of Roma in their communities
- 36 per cent believe that Roma should be forced to live separately.

Consider this: prejudice and tolerance

It may suit the purposes of some politicians and some parts of the media to reflect people's prejudice against travellers. Tolerance and mutual respect result from people knowing each other as individuals. But that is hard to do when travellers are on the move. What can be done to improve our understanding?

In Slovakia, some towns have banned Roma people altogether. Housing, schools, and even cemeteries are **segregated**, and many Roma are unemployed. Roma children are three times more likely to die in their first year of life than other Slovak children.

Several Eastern European countries with large Roma minorities, including Slovakia, joined the European Union in 2004. There was alarm in some of the more prosperous members of the Union, such as Britain, that thousands of Roma would be able to **migrate** freely to escape persecution, and claim welfare benefits.

New Age travellers

New Age travellers define themselves not just by their **nomadic** way of life, but also by their beliefs. They reject the way of life of the settled majority population in prosperous countries. This does not win them friends among the majority. New Age travellers look different and their ideas are different. People in settled, conventional communities sometimes react with hostility when large numbers of New Age travellers arrive and set up camp.

A Roma girl from Romania, where her people suffer discrimination.

Rights

Life is hard for **nomads**, especially **hunter-gatherers**. Not many of them live to old age, because they are vulnerable to fatal accidents and illnesses. Their education is often limited to the learning that can be passed on by word of mouth. Do they have the same rights as other people?

What rights?

In some countries people have rights to good health care and education. They also have civil rights such as freedom of expression and the right to vote. But very few people in poor countries have good health care and education, and in many poor countries there are few civil rights. Most **hunter-gatherer** and **pastoral** people live in poor countries, so there is less contrast between their rights and the rights of other citizens.

Schools and hospitals

Modern standards of health care and education usually involve permanent buildings and expensive equipment for schools and hospitals. How can nomads benefit from these services? Perhaps the children could stay in boarding schools, while their parents continue to move around. How can nomads travel to hospital quickly when they need treatment? It is easy to see how much more convenient it would be if they settled down near the schools and hospitals.

Rights and duties

Together with rights come duties. For example, we have a duty to obey the law and pay taxes. Few governments would be prepared to provide rights for nomadic people without making sure that they perform their duties. It is hard to keep track of your citizens if they move around. It is also hard to tax people who have an independent way of life and rarely handle money. In many places around the world, governments are encouraging or forcing nomadic people to settle down, get a job, pay taxes, and send their children to school.

Travellers' sites in Britain

Local councils in Britain provide sites for travellers to park their caravans. Some sites are well-maintained, providing water and toilets and enabling travellers' children to go to local schools. These sites are usually fenced off from the rest of the community, next to railway tracks, roads, or factories where no one else wants to live and where they cannot be seen. Other sites do not even have a water supply or toilets. Councils have no legal duty to provide sites at all.

I don't care about infrastructure. What I miss is the land. We were forced out of the reserve with our children and none of them are attending school. We'd like our children to go to school, but on our ancestral land. Only our land can teach our children both education and culture – the things that are important to us. Here there is nothing to do. We are very sad and we only think of going back home.

Children of a San community, wearing clothes and living in a government camp, risk losing touch with their traditional way of life.

The San of Botswana

As recently as the 1950s, several groups of San (formerly known as Bushmen) still lived by hunting and gathering in Namibia and Botswana. The government of Botswana set up settlements with water, clinics, and schools, and encouraged the San to move to them. They also provided water supplies in places where the San kept their traditional way of life. But later the government's actions began to look more like persecution. They set out to remove the 1500 San living in the Central Kalahari Game Reserve, to make way for nature conservation, tourism, and diamond mining. In 2004, a visitor to a former San community in this area reported that the water supply had been removed. The San were forced into government settlements.

Consider this: a hard choice

It seems that nomads have a hard choice. They can try to keep as much as possible of their traditional way of life, but miss out on the education, health care, and other rights enjoyed by settled people. Or they can have education and health care, but lose their way of life. Can a balance be achieved?

Threats

Nomads have always lived on the edge. A hard winter, or a dry summer, could bring a tribe close to **extinction**. In modern times they also face other threats.

Harsh environments

Hunter-gatherers and **pastoralists** have been confined to cold, dry, or rocky **environments** ever since farmers took over the better land. Because hunter-gatherers are always on the move, they cannot store reserves of food from good years to help them survive bad years. Pastoralists build up their herds in good years, but that only means that they can afford to lose animals in a bad year. And their herds are also vulnerable to **epidemics** of animal disease. If they lose too many animals to **drought** or disease, or have to sell them to buy food, they may not have enough animals to build up the herds again.

Disturbing the balance

Some attempts to help pastoralists create new problems. Improving the health of their animals, for instance by vaccinating them against disease, seems a good idea. But if too many animals survive, the herds become too big for the available land. This leads to **over-grazing**. Drilling boreholes to provide water can lead to over-grazing in the area around the new water supply. Improving human health can also disturb the balance between people and their environment. Some environments can only support a small number of people, and high death rates have kept human numbers down.

Settlers

As we have seen, farmers have already pushed people with nomadic ways of life into the margins. Now farmers are trying to settle in some of the last areas left to nomads. Population growth and poverty push people into the rainforests of Amazonia and Indonesia, looking for land to farm. The new settlers displace the hunter-gatherer tribes living in the rainforests. The Jumma people of the Chittagong Hill Tracts in Bangladesh live by **shifting cultivation.** Between 1977 and 1987, about 300,000 settlers from Bengal moved into their area, taking over the best land.

Consider this: temptations

The nomadic way of life is threatened by the attraction of what may seem an easier, modern lifestyle. If most young nomadic people want to live in a city, have a job, and join the majority population, the traditional way of life will die out.

Disease

Isolated people are vulnerable to epidemics of diseases caught from settlers. They have no immunity to these new diseases, so their death rates can be very high. In the winter of 1902, a sailor from a whaling ship landed on Southampton Island in the Canadian Arctic. He was suffering from dysentery. The Inuit people living on the island caught the disease, and 51 out of 56 of them died.

Economic development

Economic growth makes countries richer, but it may also damage or destroy the places where nomadic people live. Logging for hardwood timber destroys the **tropical** rainforests. Cutting timber also affects the reindeer herders of the forests of Siberia. Mining and oilfields displace people and pollute the environment. Pollution in rivers can kill off the fish that hunter-gatherers rely on for food.

In many countries, dams are seen as a key to economic growth. But the huge lakes behind the dams often submerge the traditional lands of people living by hunter-gathering or shifting cultivation. In drier areas of the world, providing **irrigation** enables farmers to settle in areas that were previously used by pastoralists.

A Chakma family. The Chakma are a tribe of the Jumma people of the Chittagong Hill Tracts in Bangladesh.

Protection

Nomadic people have distinctive, ancient, and varied lifestyles and **cultures**. They live in harmony with a wide range of **environments**, many of them very harsh. And nearly all of them are under threats of one kind or another. Should they be protected? If so, how?

Isolation

The most extreme form of protection would be isolation. This would prevent all contact with the outside world, to leave the protected tribe safe from anything that might endanger, damage, or change it. This isolation would also deny them any of the benefits that they might get from contact with the outside world. They would not be able to use modern **technology** or medicine. They would be in a sort of human zoo. Few people would seriously propose such an extreme form of protection. In practice it would not work. Outside pressures would break through, sooner or later.

Integration

At the other extreme, some people argue that it is impossible to protect nomadic people from the outside world. These people, whom they often describe as primitive or backward, should be integrated into society as quickly as possible. They should learn the national language, settle in villages and towns, take jobs on farms or in factories, live in permanent houses, and enjoy the benefits of civilization. In practice this is what often happens. Too often, nomadic people who try to merge into mainstream society get the worst-paid jobs, or no jobs at all. They also face prejudice and **discrimination** because they are different.

Survival

Most nomadic people, faced with pressures and threats from the outside world, steer a middle course between isolation and integration.

Nomadic people sometimes use modern technology. This Ndebele girl in Africa is using a mobile phone.

People from a nomadic background can live and work in settled communities. This Aboriginal woman is a health worker at a clinic in Ramingining, a community of Aboriginal people in Australia.

They can take up a settled way of life, benefit from health care and education, and use modern technology. At the same time, they keep their traditional languages, beliefs, and customs.

The Macuxi Indians of Brazil live in permanent houses, wear the same clothes as most Brazilians, and attend schools and clinics. But the clinics offer traditional herbal medicines as well as modern drugs. The communities train their own teachers, who teach the children in the Macuxi language as well as in Portuguese (the national language of Brazil). Because they can speak Portuguese, the leaders of the Macuxi can defend their rights in the country's courts. Brazil's **constitution** lays down the rights of the **indigenous** people. It says Indian lands should be **demarcated**, giving them a legal right to protect them against settlers, loggers, and gold-miners. The Macuxi, and other Brazilian Amazon tribes, press the government to demarcate their lands and give them this protection.

Tourism

Tourists from rich countries want to see different, exotic people and their traditional ways of life. Income from tourists helps some nomadic people to survive. It also gives them an extra reason to keep their culture and traditions. Many poor countries are realising that their nomadic communities bring in tourists, and this is another reason not to push for complete integration.

Consider this:
outside help

Nomadic people trying to defend their land, their rights, and their culture are not alone. Many people in rich countries agree that it is important to defend tribal people, with their distinctive culture. There are organizations that help tribal people to campaign, use the courts, and run their own schools, so that they can keep their identity.

Learning from each other

Not all contacts with settled people are disasters for **nomads**. Nomadic people can learn many useful things from settled people. If they wish, they can gain the benefits of modern science, **technology**, and medicine. Settled people can also learn from nomads, and find out more about them.

One world

Nowadays millions of tourists from rich countries visit faraway places to see different ways of life. Even without travelling, you can learn about different people's lifestyles through books, television, and the Internet. At the same time, **migration** from poor countries into rich ones creates a multi-cultural society. People can get to know **immigrants** from different **cultures**, and adopt the elements of those cultures that appeal to them. We can learn from other lifestyles, even if we do not choose them for ourselves.

Eco-tourists visiting the Qae Qare Game Farm in Botswana. Their guide is from the San D'Kar Bushman community.

Caring for the environment

Hunter-gatherers and **pastoralists** are intensely aware of their **environment**. They treat it with care and respect, and take no more than they need. Their lives depend on knowing every useful plant and animal, how to find water, how to read the signs of the weather, which plants can heal, and which are poisonous. Some modern medicines are based on plants that nomads found useful in healing.

Learning to care

Settled people have a lot to learn from nomads about respecting and nurturing the environment. The modern, industrialized, **urbanized** way of life of rich countries puts a huge strain on the environment. People consume resources from all over the world, use enormous amounts of energy, and pollute the air and water. Environmental organizations campaign for changes in government policies, and in individual lifestyles, to reduce the damage to the environment. They take inspiration from the values of nomadic people.

Environmentalists also campaign to protect some of the last unspoiled places on Earth, especially the **tropical** rainforests. Hunter-gatherers have lived in the forests for tens of thousands of years without damaging them. Logging, mining, oil extraction, ranching, and farming all destroy the forests and the people who live there.

Sharing with each other

Nomads, especially hunter-gatherers, may not have many possessions, but what they have is shared within the family or group of families who travel together. Today the group eats an animal caught by the men. Next week the men will be glad to eat the roots which the women know how to find and dig up.

Modern, industrialized countries are much richer than hunter-gatherers, but share their wealth much less evenly. There is a huge and growing gap between rich and poor countries, and between rich and poor people within countries. Poor people often live like hunter-gatherers. They find food in rubbish bins and sleep under cardboard boxes. But unlike traditional hunter-gatherers, they do not have the support of a family group.

These Amazonian rainforest Indians in Ecuador are protesting about environmental damage caused by oil drilling.

chapter six

Conclusion

Respect

For many years, people in the settled, industrialized, powerful and prosperous countries despised and patronised **nomadic** people. They considered them things of the past, primitive or backward. But, as we have seen, nomads deserve respect for the variety of ingenious ways they have found to survive and prosper in places where most of us would not last long. Travellers, too, especially seasonal workers, deserve respect for the valuable work they do for settled people.

Contempt

Mistrust and contempt for nomadic peoples has persisted for many years.

- In 1872 the government of the USA's Indian Commissioner stated: "No one certainly will rejoice more heartily than the present commissioner when the Indians of this country cease to be in a position to dictate, in any form or degree, to the government, when, in fact, the last hostile **tribe** becomes reduced to the condition of suppliants for charity."
- In 1904 a British **colonial** official in Kenya wrote: "There can be no doubt that the Maasai and many other tribes must go under. It is a prospect which I view with ... a clear conscience."
- In 1985 an Indonesian government minister, talking about the policy of settling Indonesian **migrants** on tribal land in Papua, said it was "probably the only way of getting stone age, primitive and backward people into the mainstream of Indonesian development."
- In 2001 an Indian lawyer, urging the forcible settlement of the Jarawa **hunter-gatherers** of the Andaman islands, said "I am civilized, and they are not civilized."

Achievements

People with the simplest **technology** and the fewest possessions have made major achievements, deserving respect. Their tools may be simple, but using them they can get everything they need from their **environment**. Their homes may be made of branches and leaves, but in them they bring up children, care for each other, and make guests welcome. They may have no written language, but by word of mouth they pass on creation myths and stories of their legendary heroes. They may have no churches or temples, but they have spiritual beliefs and reverence for their gods. They may be at the mercy of their environment, but it has survived for many thousands of years in their care.

Nomadic people survive in some of the harshest environment on Earth. These Tibetan nomads live on the cold, dry Tibetan plateau, within sight of the Himalayan mountains.

Wisdom

"Friends, it has been our misfortune to welcome the white man. We have been deceived. He brought with him some shining things that pleased our eyes; he brought weapons more effective than our own. Above all he brought the spirit-water [alcohol] that makes one forget old age, weakness and sorrow. But I wish to say to you that if you wish to possess these things for yourselves, you must begin anew and put away the wisdom of your fathers. You must lay up food and forget the hungry. When your house is built, your store-room filled, then look around for a neighbour whom you can take advantage of and seize all he has." Chief Red Cloud of the Oglala Sioux.

The Ogala Sioux were a tribe of Native Americans who hunted buffalo on the Great Plains. They lost their land and livelihood to white settlers.

Consider this:
the damage done

Some nomadic people, and nomadic lifestyles, have disappeared or changed for ever. Their languages, myths, beliefs, customs, and crafts cannot be brought back. But with more respect, the remaining nomadic peoples can survive in harmony with other, settled, ways of life. They can join mainstream society at their own pace if they wish. Cultures can borrow and learn from each other, without losing their identity.

Some nomadic peoples

These are some of the surviving nomadic peoples around the world. The map on pages 48–49 shows where they live.

Who are they?	Where do they live?	How do they live?	How many are there?
Hunter-gatherers			
Inuit	Canadian Arctic and Greenland	hunter-gatherers	50,000 in Canada, 55,000 in Greenland
Innu	Labrador, Canada	Some still live by hunting and fishing.	20,000
Bushmen	southern Africa	hunter-gatherers, and now pastoralists	90,500
Kanoê	Brazil	hunter-gatherers	a few dozen
Yanomami	Brazil and Venezuela	hunter-gatherers	27,000
Yora	Peru	hunter-gatherers	1000
Aboriginal people	Australia	Many live in towns or work on farms, but some still live by hunting and gathering.	250,000
Shifting cultivators			
Degar (Montagnards)	mountains of Vietnam	shifting cultivators	a few hundred thousand
Jumma	Chittagong Hill Tracts, Bangladesh	shifting cultivators	600,000
Mentawi	Siberut island, Indonesia	shifting cultivators	18,000
Macuxi	Roraima, Brazil	farmers	a few thousand

Who are they?	Where do they live?	How do they live?	How many are there?
Pastoralists			
Khanty	Siberia, Russia	herding reindeer	22,500
Saami	Arctic edge of Norway, Finland, Russia, and Sweden	Some still live by herding reindeer	35,000
Tibetan nomads	Himalayas, on the borders of China, India, Nepal, and Bhutan	pastoralists	2 million
Bedouin	deserts of North Africa and the Middle East	pastoralists, though some have settled down	about 1 million
Bakhatiar	Iran	pastoralists	800,000
Maasai	Kenya and Tanzania Sahara Desert in Africa	pastoralists	300,000
Mbororo	Sahel of Africa — between the Sahara and the rainforest	pastoralists	1.85 million in Cameroon alone
Ndebele	South Africa and Zimbabwe	farmers and pastoralists	hundreds of thousands
Tuareg	edge of the Sahara Desert in Africa	pastoralists	1–3 million

Roma	worldwide, but especially Eastern Europe	It varies, some are settled.	12 million

Where in the world?

This map of the world shows where the nomadic people described in this book live.

N

Arctic Circle

Tropic of Cancer

Equator

Tropic of Capricorn

Antarctic Circle

Inuit

Inuit

Innu

NORTH AMERICA

NORTH ATLANTIC OCEAN

Yanomami, Macuxi

Yora

Kanoê

SOUTH AMERICA

SOUTH ATLANTIC OCEAN

PACIFIC OCEAN

0   5000 km
0   2500 miles

ARCTIC

Saami

Khanty

EUROPE

ASIA

PACIFIC OCEAN

Bakhtiari

Bedouin

Tibetan
Nomads

Bedouin

Jumma

Degar
(Montagnards)

Tuareg

Mbororo

AFRICA

Maasai

Mentawi

AUSTRALASIA

Aboriginal
People

Ndebele

Bushmen

INDIAN OCEAN

SOUTHERN OCEAN

ANTARCTICA

Timeline of key events

8000–9000 BC	people begin to take up farming
about AD 370	**pastoral** Huns clash with Ostrogoth people and push them into the Roman Empire
895	Magyars settle in Hungary
11th century	Roma start their **migration** from India to Europe
13th century	Mongols invade China and Europe
13th century	Ottoman Turks settle in Turkey
1492	Columbus reaches the **New World**. European diseases start to kill millions of Native Americans. European settlers start to arrive, replacing **hunter-gatherer** people.
1788	first British colony is established in Australia. There are about 750,000 Aboriginal people there, mainly living by hunting and gathering. They soon suffer from new diseases, and settlers occupy their land.
1830	in the USA the Indian Removal Act moves 60,000 Native Americans from the southern Appalachians to a **reservation** west of the Mississippi.
1876	last Aboriginal person of Tasmania dies
1887	in the USA the Indian Allotment Act creates reservations for Native Americans. Between 1887 and 1934 they lose 86 million acres of land.
1890	in the USA army soldiers kill nearly 300 Native American men, women, and children at the Battle of Wounded Knee. This marks the end of Native American resistance to settlers taking their land.
1911	White settlers take land on the Laikipia plateau in Kenya, and expel Maasai herdsmen.
1916	Ishi, last survivor of Yahi hunter-gatherer people of California, died
1924	in the USA Native Americans are given US citizenship
1928	in Australia 31 Aboriginal people are killed in the Northern Territory

1934	in the USA the Indian Reorganization Act recognizes tribal authority and protects land held by Native Americans
1952	Indonesia begins to move people from its crowded islands, such as Java, on to other islands occupied by hunter-gatherers
1967	Australia gives the vote to Aboriginal people and counts them in the census
1971	in Australia Neville Bonner becomes the first Aboriginal person to win a seat in the Senate
1979	in Bangladesh the Population Transfer Plan is launched. Hundreds of thousands of landless Bengali people move into the Chittagong Hill Tracts, taking land from the Jumma people.
1988	in Brazil a new constitution guarantees the rights of **indigenous** people, many of them **nomadic** hunter-gatherers.
2004	the President of Brazil signs a law that creates two large new reserves for indigenous people in the Brazilian state of Para, in Amazonia. This will protect 2 million hectares (5 million acres) of forest. Illegal loggers and settlers will be forced to leave the reserves.

Glossary

Asia Minor   the part of Asia now occupied by Turkey

boomerang   hunting device used by Australian Aboriginal people, made from a piece of curved wood. A boomerang comes back to the thrower if he misses his target.

castration   removing a male animal's testicles to make it sexually inactive. This alters the animal's behaviour in ways that suit farmers and pastoralists.

colony   country ruled by the government of another, more powerful, country

constitution   rules by which a country's government is set up and works

culture   the technology, customs, ideas, beliefs, and art of a group of people

demarcate   to legally define a boundary

discriminate   treat a group of people unfairly beause they are seen as different or inferior

domesticate   to tame a wild animal, so it can be used as a farm animal

drought   long period of time, lasting many months or even years, where there is little or no rainfall

economic migrants   people who migrate for economic reasons

economy   a country's economy is created by the work people do, the money they spend, and the goods and services they produce

environment   everything around us, both natural and man-made: soil, air, water, plants and animals, buildings, farms, and factories

epidemic   when an infectious disease spreads quickly and completely through a population of people or animals

extinction   dying out. When the last of a species, or the last member of a human tribe dies, the species or tribe becomes extinct.

game   birds and animals that people hunt for food

grassland   an area of land where only grass grows. Such areas are usually too dry for permanent agriculture, so they are used by pastoralists.

hunter-gatherers   people who hunt animals, catch fish, and gather plant foods. They move around with the seasons to find food.

immigrant   someone who migrates into a country

indigenous   the people who were originally living in a particular area before the arrival of settlers and migrants from elsewhere

irrigation   supplying water for agriculture, either to grow crops where none were possible or to grow more crops by creating a more reliable supply of water

migrant   someone who migrates out of a country

migration the movement of people, especially in large numbers, from one country to another, or from one part of a country to another

New World North, South, and Central America

nomads people whose way of life depends on moving, sometimes day by day, or with the seasons

over-grazing grazing animals eating the grass or other pasture faster than it can regrow. This can kill off the pasture completely.

pastoralists people whose way of life depends on flocks and herds of animals. They move around with the seasons and to find water and grazing.

pasture vegetation eaten by grazing animals, especially domesticated animals herded by pastoralists. Pasture is usually grass, but can include other plants.

pilgrimage journey to a holy place for your religion. Some Christians go on pilgrimage to Rome. Many Muslims go on pilgrimage to Mecca.

reservation area set aside for a group of people to live in, especially for Native Americans in the USA

savannah vegetation that grows in areas of low, seasonal rainfall. Savannah vegetation is grassland with occasional trees.

segregate to keep separate

shifting cultivation farming by clearing an area of forest, growing crops for a few years, then moving on to a new area and allowing the old plot to regrow as forest

technology the tools and machines which people use to make a living and manage the environment

tipi tent made with animal skins, used by Native American hunter-gatherers in the Great Plains

transhumance moving grazing animals back and forth between summer pastures, often high in the mountains, and winter pastures, often in the valleys and plains

travellers in this book, travellers are people who are always on the move, but who are not hunter-gatherers or pastoralists

tribe group of people who share a language and culture, and live in an area of land which is smaller than a country. "Tribal" is often used to describe people with simple technology, who are often hunter-gatherers or pastoralists.

tropics area of the world between the Tropic of Cancer and the Tropic of Capricorn. The climate in the tropics is hot all the year round. Some parts of the tropics are very dry, others have very high rainfall.

urban city and town environments

wigwam dome-shaped hut covered in bark over a framework of sticks, used by Native American hunter-gatherers in the Great Plains

Further resources

Places to visit

Visit any ethnographical or anthropological museum to see artefacts made and used by tribal people, many of them migrants. For example:

British Museum, Department of Ethnography, London

Glasgow City Museums

Leeds City Museum

Manchester Museum, Manchester

Museum of Mankind, London

Pitt Rivers Museum, Oxford

University Museum of Archaeology and Anthroplogy, Cambridge

Ulster Museum, Belfast

Websites

Survival International campaigns for the rights of tribal people, many of whom are hunter-gatherers, pastoralists, or shifting cultivators.
www.survival-international.org

Many development agencies work with pastoral people, for example:
www.oxfam.org.uk

Christian Aid have web pages on pastoralist goats and the people who rely on them:
www.christian-aid.org.uk/learn/goats

Environmental organizations campaign to protect the unspoiled areas of the world where hunter-gatherers still live:
www.greenpeace.org.uk
www.foe.org.uk

There are many websites for people planning gap years, for example:
www.planetwise.net
www.gapyear.com

www.immi.gov.au
Department of Immigration and Multicultural and Indigenous Affairs in Australia

www.immigration.museum.vic.gov.au
Website for the Immigration Museum in Melbourne, Australia

Further Reading

Encyclopedia of People, (Dorling Kindersley, 2003)

Bowden, Rob, *Just the Facts: World Poverty,*
(Heinemann Library, 2002)

Collier, Martin; Marriott, Bill, *Colonisation and Conflict 1750–1990,*
(Heinemann, 2002)

Dalton, Dave, *People on the Move: Economic Migrants,*
(Heinemann Library, 2006)

Dalton, Dave, *People on the Move: Environmental Migrants,*
(Heinemann Library, 2006)

Dalton, Dave, *People on the Move: Refugees and Asylum Seekers,*
(Heinemann Library, 2006)

Darlington, Robert, *Nations of the World: Australia,*
(Raintree, 2000)

Green, Jen, *Nations of the World: Mexico,* (Raintree, 2003)

Hibbert, Adam, *Just the Facts: Globalization,*
(Heinemann Library, 2005)

Hook, Jason, *People Who Made History,* (Hodder, 2001)

Sheehan, Sean, *Just the Facts: Genocide,* (Heinemann Library, 2005)

Ure, John, *In Search of Nomads,* (Constable, 2003)

Index

Titles in the *People on the Move* series include:

Hardback 0431 01382 9

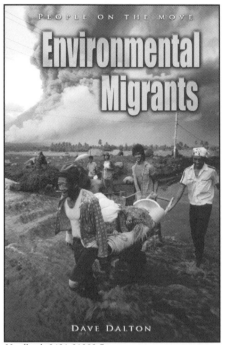

Hardback 0431 01383 7

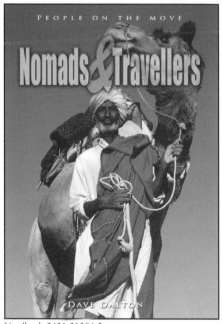

Hardback 0431 01384 5

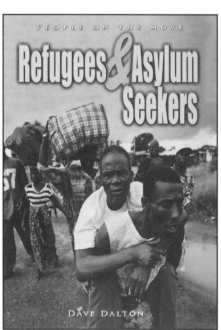

Hardback 0431 01385 3

Find out about other Heinemann Library titles on our website www.heinemann.co.uk/library